WAITING FOR THE HOST

A PLAY FOR STAGE OR STREAM IN TWO PARTS

BY MARC PALMIERI

★

DRAMATISTS
PLAY SERVICE
INC.

2

For one of the many it took from us, Thomas A. Ramsay,
January 1, 1955–April 24, 2020

WAITING FOR THE HOST (Part I) had its world premiere under the title *Streaming Passion* at Penn State Centre Stage Virtual (Rick Lombardo, Artistic Director) on April 16, 2020. It was directed by Rick Lombardo, the technical director was Chris Swetcky, the director of marketing was Cheri Sinclair, and the production stage manager was Rowan Young. The cast was as follows:

THEODORE	Steve Snyder
BEN	Cole Harris
EFFIE	Barbara Korner
VINCENT	Gabriel Peña
SARA	Julia Chereson
GRACE	Rachel Harker

STILL WAITING (Part II) had its world premiere at the Redhouse Arts Center (Hunter Foster, Artistic Director; Samara Hannah, Executive Director) in Syracuse, New York, through its "Virtual Redhouse" platform in June 2020. It was directed by Hunter Foster, the marketing and publicity was by Sue McKenna and Stephanie Consroe, the education director was Marguerite Mitchell, the video editing and graphic design were by Joshua Reid, the production manager was Daniel Whiting, and the production stage manager was Margot Reed. The cast was as follows:

THEODORE	Steve Gamba
BEN	Brendan Didio
EFFIE	Jennifer Cody
VINCENT	Robert Denzel Edwards
SARA	Marguerite Mitchell
GRACE	Yarissa Tiara Millan
DODD	Jeremy Kushnier

AUTHOR'S NOTE

Please know that Parts I and II can be produced together, as just Part I, or in whatever sequence works best. (The initial productions were done in two separate runs, Part I then Part II, as perhaps anything over an hour is a wee bit long at the laptop screen.) They have been performed both entirely live and entirely prerecorded. The play has also been staged physically, in the flesh, actors apart on the stage, in screened-off areas representing their place of sequestration.

Gender and age range is totally flexible and only suggested here; actors can be any ethnicity. Please make all that your own. Embracing the unpredictable nature of attempting to put on a play from however many separate locations at once is entirely encouraged. Making any adjustments to fit casting or technological capability is also encouraged and expected.

I live in Queens, which was referred to often as the "epicenter" of the American coronavirus outbreak. I wrote this play, both parts, alone in my basement during the "quarantine."

Part I would go live as the inaugural show of Penn State Centre Stage's virtual platform. It was the final night of Passover, 2020, at 7 P.M. The cast had rehearsed and would perform from their homes separated by hundreds of miles along the East Coast. Through my and the New York City actors' windows, we could hear people cheering in the streets for our first responders. To our delight, some thousand people arrived online at "curtain time" (or "window time") as audience members to a new, somewhere-in-between-theatre-and-live-television form. We were all in the same room, so to speak, only not. We were all together, only not. Actress Julia Chereson, who was playing Sara, just after we bid one another broken legs and went to "places," said, "I needed this." Hear, hear. Theatres had gone dark, shows closed, and yet we somehow made it to an opening night. It felt like we were doing what we loved doing, and we all indeed needed it very much.

My great thanks to my friends and family, too many to name, who encouraged me to send this to my agent, Mary Harden, and Robert Vaughan at Dramatists Play Service. Thanks to Rick Lombardo for being the first to do this thing, and to Hunter Foster, who came up with the title and told me to write Part II. Thanks to Pangdemonium in Singapore, whose production showed us just how globally shared this quarantine is. And thanks to Raven Snook, who first told the world about it in one of her heroic, daily TDF Stages articles that told people where to click to have some kind of theatre, even in its absence. Thanks to Fr. Larry Byrne, Susan and Teddy Byrne, the vestry, and the real All Saints Church in Bayside. Thanks to the Theatre Project's Mark Spina and Rev. Jason Haddox, Mercy College, and to all who've done this show. Thanks to all who will. And thanks to those who do this play someday in the future, long after this season of things so unwelcome has come to its most welcome end, and our lives, and theatres, have been resurrected.

Marc Palmieri
Summer 2020
New York City

CHARACTERS

THEODORE

BEN

EFFIE

VINCENT

SARA

GRACE

DODD

"I had else been perfect,
Whole as the marble, founded as the rock,
As broad and general as the casing air.
But now I am cabined, cribbed, confined, bound in
To saucy doubts and fears."

— William Shakespeare
The Tragedy of Macbeth

WAITING FOR THE HOST

PART I:
WAITING FOR THE HOST

Setting: The internet.
At rise: April 2020. It is 7:04 P.M. on the last night of Passover,
and late in the Christian season of Lent. On a computer screen,
five windows are open. In the windows we see Theodore (male,
50s), the rector of a small church on Long Island; Vincent
(male, 30s), a gym teacher and coach, wearing what looks
like a windbreaker; Ben (male, early 20s), a college student
and Theodore's son; Grace (female, 30s–60s); and a black
screen that just reads "Effie" across it. It may or may not be
immediately clear that Ben and Theodore are in the same
location, which is the church property. The sound of some mix
of outdoor clapping, cheering, banging on tin pans, horns, and
whistles, fading from its climax, can be heard. Grace, Theodore,
and Vincent are clapping along to what's left of the noise.

GRACE. *(Enjoying the noise.)* It gets a little louder on my block
every night. Two nights ago only a few houses were doing it. Now
it sounds like twenty!

VINCENT. Same here. Some neighbors who've never even seen
each other are banging on stuff and waving at each other through
their windows. Seven o'clock, every night. My sister said in the city,
First Avenue was so loud the EMTs in front of NYU couldn't hear
themselves saying "Thank you."

GRACE. It's inspiring.

THEODORE. And it's deserved.

EFFIE'S WINDOW. I can't figure it out! I can see y'all but I can't
see a camera!

BEN. Effie, it should be bottom left. There may be a red slash through it, and it should say, "Allow camera" or "Start video" or—

EFFIE'S WINDOW. A red slash?

THEODORE. It's an icon.

EFFIE'S WINDOW. An icon?

BEN. Not like a religious icon, just a camera icon.

EFFIE'S WINDOW. I don't know what you're talking about.

GRACE. She doesn't use the computer much.

EFFIE'S WINDOW. No, I use the computer, Grace. I check email sometimes but this is…

THEODORE. Ben, make sure she knows she's not looking for a real camera.

BEN. I know, Dad. Effie?

EFFIE'S WINDOW. Yeah?

BEN. So you're looking not at the actual lens of your PC, but the camera symbol—

> *Suddenly, Effie's window brightens and we see Effie, female, 50s–70s, looking baffled.*

ALL. Effie! There she is!

> *Effie's window goes black again, saying only: "Effie." Everyone groans.*

VINCENT. Damn. We had her.

EFFIE'S WINDOW. Can you see me?

ALL. NO!

BEN. But we saw you for a second.

EFFIE'S WINDOW. You did? Wait a second. Oh, this is aggravating!

THEODORE. Relax. Our Jesus is running late.

VINCENT. Running late?

THEODORE. Our one professional performer.

VINCENT. That's a stretch. And how do you "run late" when you live in a one-room place and your appointment is in your one chair?

GRACE. I haven't seen Sara in years.

Grace clears her throat.

She was in two of my classes. She's so talented. I'm not surprised she's in New York City. And busy.

VINCENT. She's not busy. Nobody's busy. It's lockdown. She wasn't busy in the first place.

BEN. Effie?

EFFIE'S WINDOW. Ben, I have no idea what—

Effie appears again, in a perfect medium closeup.

—you're talking about. Icon, slash. Can I do this any other way?

ALL. We see you! Effie you're on!

EFFIE. What?

THEODORE. Keep it right there! That's perfect!

EFFIE. I'm on?

BEN and THEODORE. Yes!

EFFIE. Somehow I got it on. Great.

The view of Effie abruptly lifts, showing only the tip of her forehead.

BEN. Well now we can't see you. But we can see your ceiling.

THEODORE. Sara should be on by now. She said five minutes late.

BEN. Effie, now you have to bend your screen toward you a bit.

EFFIE. Bend my screen? Won't it break? It's glass.

BEN. *Tilt*, I should say. *Tilt* the screen back to the way you had it. There should be some kind of joint—

VINCENT. You just tilted it up, now tilt it back *down*, Effie.

EFFIE. Ah, I see. You mean—

She tilts herself back into view.

BEN. Yes! Hands off now! RELEASE!

She does, startled.

EFFIE. Oh y'all can see what I see, is that it?

BEN. That is it.

THEODORE. So while we wait for Sara does anyone have any questions? We have our casting set?

GRACE. It's the same script we do every year, right?

THEODORE. Right. A few casting changes, though, to streamline, keep this thing doable.

GRACE. Usually we have the whole vestry perform.

THEODORE. Well…usually we do it live on Palm Sunday too, but we didn't.

BEN. There's nothing "usual" anymore.

VINCENT. Like bringing in a ringer who not only isn't a parishioner, but who is Jewish.

GRACE. Well, it's Passover, too.

THEODORE. Our church is open to all. Vincent, you promised me you two were on good terms.

GRACE. Oh there's a history! Gossip! Spill it!

EFFIE. You know, Father, I think this whole season has been a true Lent. This virus. True suffering. It feels like a few weeks ago we were talking about what we'd give up for Lent. I was gonna give up cheese. Then we gave up civilization. And I've had more cheese than I've had in my whole life.

THEODORE. Well I am glad we're doing this. And so will our parishioners be. More and more have been tuning in to our streaming masses, for which I'm very grateful. After our "Digital Palm Sunday" I got a bunch of messages saying how much they missed the Passion performance. That's why we're doing this. The closer to normal, the better for everyone.

VINCENT. So this will be recorded?

BEN. Yes. I'll edit it and put it on our website.

VINCENT. And we can enjoy the crucifixion all year long!

THEODORE. Thanks to Ben. My son's misfortune of being dragged home from SUNY Albany gives us a chance to use his media skills. I call him Ben C. DeMille.

BEN. *(Not laughing.)* That's hilarious, Dad.

GRACE. Jesus is a girl. That's different. And Jewish. I like it!

THEODORE. Well…

VINCENT. Who's gonna say it?

EFFIE. Say what?

VINCENT. "The real Jesus was Jewish!"

GRACE. That's right! Everybody was Jewish back then.

BEN. That's not correct.

THEODORE. I saw her father at 7-Eleven, who is actually a gentleman I went to high school with. Through a mask he made out of a scarf, he started telling me about Sara and that she was feeling very down, and that the theatre business is being hit so hard with all this. Obviously. And he also told me he had a friend…an older man who, just that morning…hours before I saw him…who had symptoms one morning and by the next night…

> *Pause.*

I didn't know what else to say…anyway, I thought this would be a nice way to involve someone else from the community. And get a skilled reader! So I told him we needed a Jesus.

VINCENT. Though we didn't *need* Jesus, since I'm usually Jesus.

THEODORE. It's a good deed, Vincent. As I said, she's been hit hard.

VINCENT. She's "hit hard" because her restaurant is doing takeout only. Not because theatre is hit hard.

GRACE. Vincent…? Do you want to share your history with Jesus before she arrives?

VINCENT. We were together, we broke up. Wasn't pretty.

EFFIE. Ooh. Did someone break a covenant? That's a Bible joke.

VINCENT. Not really. What's a covenant again?

THEODORE. Are you kidding me?

VINCENT. Yes! I'm kidding. Not really.

THEODORE. God made covenants with the His people, agreements. Contracts. He'd look out for them if they were loyal, praised him, lived under his rules…and God's side of the covenant was…well, he wouldn't destroy mankind.

> *Silence. People stare, shuffle papers, think…*

VINCENT. Anyway, I haven't seen her in a long time. I liked Sara a lot. I turned against her when she could have saved me. Bible joke.

Effie's screen goes black. "Effie."

BEN. EFFIE WHAT DID YOU DO!

EFFIE'S WINDOW. I hit the icon with my pinky.

She returns.

Sorry.

Another window opens. It's black, with "Sara: SAG-AFTRA Eligible" across it.

GRACE. Jesus has appeared!

VINCENT. Late, but we'll take it!

Sara, 30s, appears.

SARA. I am so, so sorry. Hello everyone! So so sorry!

THEODORE. Hello Sara!

SARA. Hi Father Theo!

EFFIE. Does she have to call you "Father" if she's Jewish?

VINCENT. Call him Rabbi.

THEODORE. We have our cast!

SARA. Hi everyone!

THEODORE. Grace, you said you know Sara from high school.

GRACE. Hello Sara!

SARA. Oh my god! Hi!

THEODORE. You know, let's go around and just say our names and who we're playing and then we can get going. Hate for this to take all night!

SARA. Well I don't mind. I'm staying up late for a dinner party of one. It's the last night of Passover and I can eat normal again.

GRACE. Why? Do they fast for Passover?

SARA. It's matzah time. My bubbe sent me a box. But on the last night you can relax. The last plague is passed, and we've been spared.

Pause.

I'm not usually observant. This year I am.

GRACE. Well I don't mind if we take all night. All I've got to do is sit here and suspect myself of symptoms.

She coughs, just a bit.

EFFIE. Ha! See? You say symptoms and suddenly you're hackin'—

Grace coughs once more. Sara covers her mouth and nose.

THEODORE. You okay Grace?

GRACE. Allergies. Don't worry!

She clears up.

THEODORE. Effie, why don't you say hello before we lose you again.

EFFIE. Nice to meet you, Sara. I'm Effie. I'm very confused.

SARA. Hi.

BEN. Tell us all what you're reading.

EFFIE. I'm reading *Love in the Time of Cholera*.

BEN. Sorry, I mean what are you reading tonight, what parts.

SARA. I read that book, it's really beautiful. I love stories about women dumping guys. Oh, hi Vincent!

EFFIE. Hold on.

Effie looks at her pages.

I'm reading a lot of parts.

VINCENT. Hello Sara.

EFFIE. I'm reading Accusers, Servant Girl, and…Disciples… Yes that's it. Whew! I'm gonna be pooped! I'm already pooped.

THEODORE. Ben?

BEN. Hello Sara, I'm Ben, son of the preacher man, snatched from my amazing sophomore year and delighted to be hanging out with my very Christian parents for the foreseeable future. I'm reading the Chief Priest, the High Priest, and also Accusers.

THEODORE. Ben is also directing. I call him Ben C.—

BEN. Please don't, Dad.

SARA. Nice to meet you Ben C.

BEN. Nice to meet you. And I'm not directing, I'm just… I'll edit it together and try to…you know…help.

THEODORE. And you've said hello to Vincent.

SARA. Didn't know you were in this, Vin.

VINCENT. It's my church.

THEODORE. For Christmas and Easter only, he means.

VINCENT. I'll be reading the key roles of Judas and Peter.

SARA. Perfect. One backstabber, one coward.

VINCENT. Why is that perfect?

SARA. See there you go. Denial number one. Peter made three, right? I know the New Testament. I took a theology core course. So get ready for some Bible jokes!

VINCENT. Everyone, just to be clear, I'm Sara's ex from the college years. I was local and she went far away to Queens College a few exits away.

SARA. Ha! Well, "ex"… I don't know. Not sure I'd give it that weight.

VINCENT. It's great to see you.

THEODORE. Grace you didn't mention who you're reading—

GRACE. Oh yes, I'm playing Pilate! Who famously washes his hands.

SARA. Good habit these days, as we all know!

THEODORE. Well…absolutely. Unless it's metaphorically.

VINCENT. Oh I think washing your hands metaphorically can be very healthy. I know I did it once.

> Vincent smirks and stares ahead, Sara does the same, he wins that round.

SARA. Well anyway, it's great to meet everyone! I'm Sara, I'm SAG-eligible, and I'm reading Jesus! I am very honored. The Jewish Bible is very important to your faith as well so I feel very close to all of you. We are all children of Abraham.

THEODORE. We are thrilled to have you and folks as I've mentioned, Sara is a real actor, so we can have our game raised!

VINCENT. That is exciting.

THEODORE. I'll be reading the Narrator. So it's simple. Ben will record us reading it through. Just come in with your lines. Hopefully you highlighted so they don't sneak up on you.

SARA. Totally highlighted!

She holds up her script. It's in a binder.

EFFIE. Highlighted?

THEODORE. And Ben, you had something you wanted to say?

BEN. Right, so folks, if you could give just a beat, just a breath before jumping in with your line. We don't want to have overlapping sound. Does that make sense? Short pause, I'm talking.

SARA. Absolutely. It's for editing purposes later. "In post" as we say!

EFFIE. A breath. I can do that.

THEODORE. Alright so folks, again, I want to say thank you. This has been an incredibly challenging time, as we all know. Last week we had almost forty people watching the streamed service which... I'm really happy about. What we plan to do here, as we said, is to have this up so people can share in our usual tradition, even if we're apart.

SARA. I have a question.

THEODORE. Of course!

SARA. Will this stay on the internet? Say, if our friends can't see it that early in the morning but want to watch me later?

VINCENT. *(Sarcastic.)* Could be good for your "actor reel," right?

THEODORE. Ben, please take that question?

Effie's screen goes black. "Effie."

GRACE. Effie's gone.

BEN. Effie you're gone again. And sure, Sara. This will all be available on our website.

SARA. Awesome thank you!

VINCENT. That's good news. Because I know all my friends will want to watch this instead of anything on Netflix.

THEODORE. Okay. Effie?

EFFIE'S WINDOW. *(To self.)* And I'm out again. Shit. This goddamn piece of shit.

BEN. Hey Effie?

GRACE. We can hear you, honey.

Effie appears again, only it's back to her forehead only.

SARA. There she is!

GRACE. Pull the camera down.

BEN. The *monitor*. And tilt it. Don't pull it!

Effie reaches at her screen and pulls herself into view.

THEODORE. Perfect! Let's get this going!

SARA. Any notes?

THEODORE. How do you mean?

SARA. Anything. I look okay? And I'm assuming we're self-consciously accepting Jesus is a woman, right? Gender neutral? Which I love. You don't want me pretending to be a guy, right? I will totally do it, but I don't think it's necessary in 2020.

THEODORE. No just be you. I mean, be Jesus, but it's you. A girl.

VINCENT. Sara, you're gonna be great as a girl.

SARA. Thanks Vincent. You too.

VINCENT. Thank you!

SARA. Is…everyone okay with you and yours, Vincent? Your family?

VINCENT. Yeah, so far. Thanks. My sister's an EMT. So it's scary. Every day. It's a nightmare, really. She has a one-year-old. But what can we do?

Silence.

SARA. If I didn't say it, because we just met, I hope everyone here is doing okay, and your families are okay, and you're all following protocol.

THEODORE. Yup. Social distancing. And here we are, social distancing, still managing to worship.

VINCENT. You look good, Sara. Social distancing suits you.

SARA. Still wearing baseball clothes huh?

VINCENT. This is a windbreaker from my baseball team. We lost our entire season. The seniors are devastated.

SARA. I'm sorry. That sucks.

THEODORE. Okay, Ben, you recording?

BEN. Hold on…

He leans out of frame a moment as if to press something.

We are recording.

Theodore, holding his script, sits erectly and addresses his camera.

THEODORE. *One of the twelve disciples, called Judas Iscariot, went to the chief priests and said:*

VINCENT. *(As Judas.) What will you give me if I betray Jesus to you?*

THEODORE. *They paid him thirty silver pieces of silver.*

VINCENT. So how much is that, like in 2020? A lotta dough?

THEODORE. Uh…

BEN. Hold. Let me cut.

VINCENT. Oh we were recording?

BEN. Yes.

VINCENT. Sorry, thought we were rehearsing first. My bad.

THEODORE. It was about twenty dollars, I think. The silver. Should we go from the top?

BEN. Hold on.

He is leaning off again.

VINCENT. Twenty bucks. I thought it was a fortune! Judas was a horrible businessman.

BEN. Let's just go from… *What will you give me…*

SARA. *(Sort of teasing.)* Vincent, do you connect with what Judas is saying? *What can I get from you,* is all he is interested in. *What can I take before ditching you?*

VINCENT. Actually, I've thought about it, Sara, and that's not really what he's doing. He's helping the story along by a necessary sacrifice. It's his role and he's playing it. Sort of like if his girlfriend had to go back to school at the end of the summer, and dorm there, even though she lives forty minutes away, and Judas said, "Let's break up so you can have your space, and I'll live at home, go to school, *and* get a job."

SARA. That comparison makes no sense.

21

THEODORE. Okay let's hit the lines and get this done.

GRACE. Yes! Let's hit it!

BEN. Go Vinny.

VINCENT. *(As Judas.) What will you give me if I betray Jesus to you?*

THEODORE. *They paid him thirty silver pieces. And then he looked for a chance to betray Jesus. Now, on the first day of the Passover, the disciples came to Jesus and said:*

> *Silence.*

Effie that's you—

> *Effie jumps right in.*

EFFIE. *(As Disciples.) Disciples. Where do you want us to make the preparations for you to eat the Passover?*

BEN. Um… Let's just take that again?

EFFIE. Yes?

BEN. Two things, Effie. Remember, I need that breath before you say your line, and you don't have to say who you are before you speak.

EFFIE. So don't say Effie? Did I do that?

BEN. No, don't say "Disciples." That's your character. Or characters. Just say the lines. After the breath.

EFFIE. Ah! Gotcha. Sorry, forgot the breath!

BEN. Okay. Dad, just take it from your last line, then Effie, your line.

EFFIE. Okay.

> *A beat.*

THEODORE. *The Disciples came to Jesus and said:*

> *Effie inhales and blows out a large, long, audible breath. Whew! Then…*

EFFIE. *(As Disciples.) Where do you want us to make the preparations—*

BEN. Okay sorry. Cut again.

> *Vincent is laughing hard, covering his face. Sara is too, but doing better hiding it. Vincent presses something to give himself a black screen for a moment. "Vincent."*

I meant a silent breath, Eff. Not a loud blowing groan.

EFFIE. Oh. Sure!

BEN. Okay.

EFFIE. Oh. I see. Ha! Hahahaha!

> *She guffaws. Grace joins. Sara smiles. Theodore and Ben remain focused.*

THEODORE. Yes. It's funny. We ready?

> *Vincent returns, almost cured of the giggles but not entirely.*

ALL. Yes.

THEODORE. *The disciples said:*

EFFIE. *(As Disciples.) Where do you want us to make the preparations for Passover?*

THEODORE. *Jesus said:*

SARA. *(As Jesus; eloquent, thoughtful.) Go to the city, to a certain man, and say to this man: Your teacher says, my time is near; I will keep the Passover at your house with my disciples.*

> *Pause.*

GRACE. Oh wow, that makes me so sad.

> *Beat.*

BEN. Cut!

THEODORE. What's wrong, Grace? You okay?

GRACE. Oh I'm sorry. Nice acting, Sara.

SARA. Thank you! It was a good take, I think.

GRACE. I was moved. I thought how sad because if this was today, nobody could possibly go to that man's house for dinner. Everyone has to be at home, alone. All these get-togethers, canceled. What Sara said just reminded me. Right now nobody can say, "I'll keep the Passover with my disciples at my house tonight."

SARA. That'd be funny to call your friends "disciples." You'd have to have some ego. *(Catches herself.)* Oh, I mean, if you did that today, now, as a regular person. Not if you're Jesus, back then. No offense to Jesus.

THEODORE. We okay, Ben?

BEN. We can pick up at your next line, Dad. We got all that.

THEODORE. Okay. Moving on.

SARA. Grace, you're right, though. It's hard. All of this. But when I look out my window and see people outside every night, just out on the streets and totally disregarding social distancing, it makes me so mad. So selfish. What is wrong with people?

VINCENT. I mean you gotta go out a little.

SARA. No. I'm sorry but you are putting people's lives in danger. Selfishness to the highest degree. "Stay at home, save lives." I put a filter on all my social networks profiles that says that over my headshot.

VINCENT. You gotta go get your stuff up at the store. You're talking about those spring breaker morons on YouTube or whatever. Regular people still have to go places. You can be careful but not totally locked inside your house. Or in your case, locked in your city-subsidized art resident building. And some still have to work. Some people have no choice.

THEODORE. Okay! Ready? Ben? Where do you want it from?

BEN. From sitting down with the twelve. It's recording.

THEODORE. Everyone ready?

SARA. Ready.

Pause, they begin.

THEODORE. *When it was evening, Jesus took his place with the twelve.*

SARA. *(As Jesus.) Truly, I tell you…one of you will…betray me.*

THEODORE. *And they became distressed and said:*

EFFIE. *Not I Lord!*

SARA. *(As Jesus.) The one who has dipped his hand into the bowl with me will betray me.*

She pauses.

Well if it's 2020 whoever dips his hands in my bowl has already more than betrayed me. He's trying to kill me. It's the hands, most of all. The overwhelming majority of people are getting it from the virus being on their hands, and they don't wash, they touch their face, and they get it.

BEN. Cut.

GRACE. I wash my hands all day. Every thirty minutes even if I've only been asleep on the sofa or touching the remote.

SARA. It's the key. The main key. Wash. Hands.

THEODORE. Absolutely. But of course this was not 2020. This was a time where they could be out and having a good time.

SARA. But it was Passover so they wouldn't really be having too good a time. It's a solemn observance. But still, the way they ate. Horrible. The Bible is full of plagues. No wonder, right?

VINCENT. I wonder if Judas was able to eat anything. He must have been shittin' bricks.

SARA. Well if we ate like this right now, sharing and touching and whatever, it would definitely be *our* last supper. Or at least we'd have like five to fourteen suppers left before symptoms.

THEODORE. So, I have a suggestion.

VINCENT. I know what it is. Let's try to act and not comment? Is that the suggestion? Let's act professionally, especially if we are SAG-eligible?

SARA. Fuck you, Vincent. Sorry everyone.

EFFIE. That's fine. I have a filthy mouth.

THEODORE. There is so much to talk about. But first we should just say exactly what's here and reserve judgment. So we can put this thing together!

SARA. Absolutely.

GRACE. Of course.

> *Effie's window goes black. "Effie."*

BEN. Effie? Gone again.

> *No response. Pause.*

Effie?

GRACE. Effie?

THEODORE. Oh man.

> *Effie pops back on, starts talking with no audio.*

BEN. Cannot hear you!

> *Effie keeps talking.*

You. Are. Muted. Microphone. Icon!

> *Ben points to the bottom right of his screen. Effie stops talking.*

For a moment, her screen goes black again. "Effie." Then, quickly, she returns with full volume.

EFFIE. This good?

ALL. Yes!/Yay!

EFFIE. Sorry I had to sneeze and I hit the camera and the microphone icons so I didn't get it all over everyone.

Sara covers her face.

SARA. Are you having symptoms, Effie?

EFFIE. No, I'm in my basement and it's dusty.

SARA. Good. So glad.

She uncovers.

THEODORE. Ben, where am I?

BEN. Well we could start with Jesus again with "The man who dipped his hand…" and infected his friends with coronavirus…

SARA. Okay.

VINCENT. And stick to the script, SAG-Awards.

SARA. I will.

VINCENT. You know, my friend is in the Screen Actors Guild. She was a cheerleader in a movie and she had to join. She gets free movies sent to her every year.

Sara is silent a moment, staring at the camera, suddenly jaundiced, without expression.

THEODORE. Okay…here's your cue. Effie just said, *Surely not I, Lord.*

Sara does not flinch.

Sara?

SARA. "Special skills."

THEODORE. Excuse me?

SARA. She got in a movie because she's on some casting director list that has people with special skills. She's probably not even an actor.

VINCENT. She's not. She's a cheerleader for the Baltimore Blast. Soccer team.

SARA. Good for her. How do you know her? Fuck it, can we move on?

THEODORE. Yes. Please. Ready Ben?

BEN. Shit yes.

THEODORE. *Not I, Lord?*

SARA. *(As Jesus.) The one who dipped his hand in my bowl with me will betray me.* Ugh. *The Son of Man does what is written, but woe to him who betrayed me. It would have been better for that one not to have been born.*

    Beat.

THEODORE. *Judas, who betrayed Jesus, said:*

VINCENT. *(As Judas.) Surely not I, Rabbi?*

THEODORE. *While they ate, Jesus took a loaf of bread, and after blessing it, broke it, gave it to his disciples—*

    Sara shakes her head in quiet disgust.

SARA. *(As Jesus, disgusted.) Take this.* Ugh. *All of you and eat.*

    She shakes her head no.

Not healthy!

THEODORE. *Then he took the cup, and after giving thanks he gave it to them, said,*

SARA. *(As Jesus.) Drink from it, all of you.*

    She pauses, really struggles.

So bad.

VINCENT. Come on, babe. No worries. You're asymptomatic.

SARA. Doesn't matter. You can carry it. You can spread it.

THEODORE. Please, Vincent.

BEN. Keep going! Just take that pause first!

    Sara takes a beat.

SARA. *(As Jesus.) Drink from it, all of you. This is my blood which will be given up for you.*

BEN. Cut.

SARA. No good?

THEODORE. Very good!

BEN. I cut because I heard sound outside. I think I heard honking outside, or agonized screaming, and I don't want to pick it up on the mic.

VINCENT. Speaking of wine, all liquor stores closed as of last night.

SARA. No. Not true.

EFFIE. Really?

SARA. Absolutely not true.

VINCENT. Governor Cuomo shut them down. Whole state. Dry as a desert.

SARA. I was in one today. That's wrong.

VINCENT. April Fools!

GRACE. Vincent! April Fools is far past!

VINCENT. Still works.

EFFIE. Whew! Scared me! My store delivers. I do a good magnum a day.

VINCENT. Sara you were out and in a store? I hope it was worth the risk you put everyone under. Get some Malbec? Your favorite? It is Malbec, yes?

SARA. You recall. Impressive. And of course I was very careful. I had a mask and my gloves and the man was very grateful I was buying his products. Small business and theatre are hit hard.

VINCENT. I am sure he was grateful, and I'm sure you were careful. It's okay you went out. No judgment. I've always trusted you. You want to get a drink?

Pause.

SARA. Sure.

Beat.

But we can't.

VINCENT. Snapchat drink. Video. Whatever we do and say is all gone afterwards.

SARA. All gone afterwards. The perfect app for you.

THEODORE. Okay everyone. Focus. Ben, we good?

BEN. *(Now wearing headphones.)* As good as we're going to get.

THEODORE. That's enough for me. Let's go.

BEN. Mount of Olives. Ready when you are. Ready all? Page three top. Grace and Effie, I'll cut you out during the night scene in the garden but stay ready. I'll bring you back on.

GRACE. Okay.   EFFIE. Got it!

ALL. Ready.

> *Effie's and Grace's windows go black. "Effie," "Grace."*

THEODORE. *They went to the Mount of Olives, and Jesus said:*

SARA. *(As Jesus.) You will all desert me. It is written. But I will be raised up.*

THEODORE. *Peter said to him:*

VINCENT. *(As Peter.) Sara, I will never desert you.*

BEN. What? He said Sara.

THEODORE. Let it go, Ben. *But Sara said:*

SARA. *(As Jesus.) Truly I tell you, before this very night, before the cock crows...*

> *Vincent puts his hand to his mouth. Sara cracks just a bit, fighting a chuckle.*

...before the cock crows, you will deny me. Three times.

VINCENT. *(Flirty.)* Three times? That's a busy cock!

SARA. *(Flirty back.)* So awful.

VINCENT. Bible jokes!

THEODORE. This is for a mass, folks!

BEN. Let's keep going. Dad? It'll be *my* agonized screaming soon.

THEODORE. Um...okay... *Peter said to him:*

VINCENT. *(As Peter; finds his place.) Even though I must die with you. I will not deny you.*

> *Sara makes an "Aw, that's sweet" face.*

THEODORE. *Then Jesus went with them into the garden.*

SARA. *(As Jesus.) Sit here while I go over there and pray.*

THEODORE. *He threw himself on the ground.*

SARA. *(As Jesus.) Father, if it is possible, let this cup pass from me!*

THEODORE. *Jesus saw that the disciples were sleeping.*

Effie's and Grace's windows illuminate. Both of their heads are slumped. They are actually asleep.

BEN. *(Hushed.)* Is that real sleeping?

VINCENT. *(Whispers.)* Shhh! Happy accident, as they say.

BEN. That kinda works! Don't wake them up!

THEODORE. *(A bit softer.)* The hour was at hand for the Son of Man to be betrayed into the hands of the Romans. Judas arrived, with him a large crowd with swords and clubs. Judas turned to the priests and said:

VINCENT. *(As Judas.)* The one I will kiss is Jesus. Arrest him.

THEODORE. At once Judas moved to Jesus, and Jesus moved to Judas.

> *Sara and Vincent stare into their cameras, as if at each other. There is something there. They would kiss, if only they could.*

VINCENT. *(As Judas; charmingly.)* Greetings.

SARA. *(As Jesus; coquettishly.)* Friend. What…are you here to do?

> *A pause.*

THEODORE. Judas kissed him.

> *Sara and Vincent, as if they've kissed, put their hands to their lips. A moment, then Sara pulls her hand away and hand-sanitizes.*

Then they laid hands on Jesus and arrested him. Then they took Jesus to the high priest, but Peter followed at a distance. Jesus heard his accusers in the courtyard, as Peter listened.

> *Pause.*

Effie?

> *Nothing.*

Accuser? Effie?

BEN. EFFIE!

EFFIE. *(Wakes.)* Oh! Hello?

> *Something bumps on her end. We see only her forehead. Grace wakes with a smile.*

GRACE. I'm sorry I dozed.

THEODORE. Page five. Bottom. Accuser. Hit it.

EFFIE. Hold on.

BEN. Page five.

Grace clears her throat, then stares off.

THEODORE. Grace?

GRACE. *(A bit spacey.)* Sorry. I'm fine. I was dreaming nice things… Seemed real. Ugh, what a…what a sad time…truly. This Lent. But this will pass. *To all things there is a season.* Right?

SARA. Right! *Ecclesiastes.* The Jewish Bible. Or in your faith, the Old Testament.

EFFIE. Alright, I'm there.

She takes her big, loud, moaning breath again.

(As Accuser.) This fellow said—

BEN. Hold, Effie. Sorry. No noise in the breath okay?

EFFIE. Oh right. I'll hold. Just say action!

BEN. Sure. I haven't said that all night but sure. And…"action!"

EFFIE. *(As Accuser.) This fellow said, "I am able to destroy the temple of God and rebuild it in three days."*

THEODORE. *The high priest stood up and said:*

BEN. *(As High Priest.) Have you no answer? What is this they testify against you? Tell us if you are the Messiah, the Son of God!*

SARA. *(As Jesus.) You have said so, but I tell you, from now you will see the Son of Man, seated at the right hand of power, coming from the clouds of…*

Sara balks.

Of Heaven.

A pause.

Heaven.

A pause.

Hmm. Haven't thought about Heaven in a while.

A pause.

THEODORE. *Then the high priests consulted, and gave their verdict.*

BEN. *(As High Priest.) He is guilty. He deserves death.*

THEODORE. *Then they slapped his face and struck him, saying, "Prophesy! Prophesy to us, Messiah!" Jesus was silent. Meanwhile, a servant girl approached Peter.*

EFFIE. *(As Servant Girl.) This is the man with Jesus of Nazareth. His friend!*

VINCENT. *(As Peter.) I do not know what you are talking about.*

THEODORE. *Another accused him.*

VINCENT. *(As Peter.) I don't know the man.*

THEODORE. *Another accused him.*

VINCENT. *(As Peter.) I do not know the man.*

THEODORE. *The cock crowed.*

> *A nice moment of pause, until Effie makes a grating sound of a rooster crow. Some chuckle, some wait a moment before Theodore keeps going.*

Soon Jesus stood before the governor, Pontius Pilate.

GRACE. *(As Pilate.) Do you not hear the accusations made against you?*

THEODORE. *Jesus gave no answer. Pilate was amazed. At the festival, he was accustomed to release one prisoner for the crowd. There was a notorious prisoner, Barabbas, and Pilate offered the crowd the freedom of Jesus or Barabbas.*

GRACE. *(As Pilate.) Whom do you want me to release for you, Barabbas, or Jesus?*

THEODORE. *And the crowd said:*

ALL. *BARABBAS!*

GRACE. *(As Pilate.) Then what should I do with Jesus who is called Messiah?*

ALL. *CRUCIFY HIM!*

GRACE. *(As Pilate.) Why? What evil has he done?*

THEODORE. *But they shouted more for crucifixion.*

GRACE. *(As Pilate.) I am innocent of this man's blood.*

THEODORE. *And Pilate washed his hands.*

SARA. Good for him.

Grace pulls out Purell and makes a show of sanitizing. Most laugh quietly with her.

THEODORE. *The Roman soldiers flogged Jesus, and put a twisted crown of thorns atop his head. They mocked him, saying, "Hail, King of the Jews!" They spat on him, struck him on the head with reed, and stripped him of his clothes. Then they took him to Golgotha, and crucified him between two thieves. And the high priests mocked him, saying:*

BEN. *(As High Priest.)* If you are the Son of God, come down from the cross, save yourself!

THEODORE. *But there was nothing. From noon to darkness. At last Jesus cried out:*

SARA. *(As Jesus; pronounces it well.)* Eloi! Eloi! Lema sabachthani?

VINCENT. Whoah. How'd you know how to pronounce that?

SARA. *(As Jesus.)* My college education, for which you resented me pursing as a campus resident. It's Greek.

VINCENT. I never resented. Well, opa!

BEN. It's actually Aramaic, and Sara can we get it again? Please don't interrupt, anyone. Almost done!

SARA. Well hold on. Should I really say this like this? Does anyone out there know what this actually means? I mean, I do! I took a core course—

THEODORE. Well they hear it every year when we do this.

SARA. Okay but... I think... I mean, it should be said in English. This moment. Frankly, it's the most amazing moment. If the story ends here, let's say...with his death, like the crowd, like I, in my tradition, think it does, it sort of makes it the most beautiful human story ever. I think.

THEODORE. What do you mean?

SARA. I mean...what an amazing last line, right? What a terrible and amazing idea, that God is gone.

THEODORE. Yes. It is. *(After a pause.)* "Father, Father...why have you...abandoned me?"

A moment. Something troubling occurs to him.

33

This is hard sometimes. It's…to do what I do.

Silence.

SARA. It must be.

THEODORE. People come to ask questions. Like your father asked me and…they ask me questions I cannot answer. I don't want to disappoint them. Tell them I have no answer. Make it worse, maybe. See, many of my parishioners are old. But so many, very old. And this thing is killing them. It is killing the older of us. And many others. Every day. It's getting worse. And there's no end in sight.

A silence.

BEN. Why don't we say the Aramaic, as usual. Then Dad, just add a line, "Which means…" and say it in English. I like the idea.

THEODORE. Well Sara should say it.

SARA. No, Father. I think you should say it.

Pause.

THEODORE. Fine. Yes. Okay.

BEN. Okay. Let's go ahead. Sara, again.

A beat.

SARA. *Eloi, Eloi…Lema sabachthani?*

THEODORE. Which means…*Father.* Which means…

Theodore looks up, off-frame, into the sky, as it were.

Father, Father…why have you abandoned me?

He raises his hands a little. A long silence.

BEN. Dad? Ready to continue?

Silence continues. Theodore is still looking up.

Dad? You okay?

Still silent, Theodore slowly brings his eyes down and into his camera lens, as if looking at all of his cast, all of the audience.

THEODORE. Everyone… We'll stop it there this year. We'll stop the story there.

A silence.

BEN. Okay… That's a wrap.

THEODORE. We'll edit it. And we will…stream it.

A pause.

Good night everyone. And Sara. Happy…Passover.

ALL. *(Staggered.)* Good night/Thank you/Night.

The cast all look straight ahead a moment. Grace sniffles once. A pause. All windows begin to black until there is only Ben and Theodore, then just Theodore, who gazes ahead, blankly, tired. It is an extended moment, then all goes black. Curtain.

End of Part I

PART II:
STILL WAITING

Scene 1

Setting: The internet.
At rise: It's just turned June 2020. In the two windows on the screen we see Ben and Vincent. They have not gotten haircuts in far too long (perhaps Vincent got hold of a clipper and took matters into his own hands). We find them in mid-conversation.

VINCENT. So we first broke up because a *good* thing was happening, which was college. Then got back together because a *bad* thing was happening, the coronavirus.

BEN. I bet the pandemic ended more relationships than it actually started. Take me, right before we had to leave school I finally got up the guts to ask out this girl, an English major I met in British Lit. I had a crush on her since the day I got to Albany.

VINCENT. You were there almost two whole years. It took that long to ask her out?

BEN. It took that long to speak to her! And she's about as shy as I am so…yeah. I was ridiculous. From what I could tell in class, she was into poetry so I started trying to write love poems. I would stick them in her mailbox unsigned.

VINCENT. Wow, you *were* ridiculous!

BEN. Well, not totally unsigned. I signed them, "Love, Me."

VINCENT. That would be hard to trace.

BEN. Finally one night she saw me at the mailbox. She knew, I figured. So I said, "Hi. It's Me." And asked her out. She said, "Me, I'd love to."

VINCENT. Must've been good poetry. She said yes.

BEN. Yeah, and our date ended up being scheduled for the night everyone had to be packed up and off campus for the lockdown.

VINCENT. I'm sorry, man. Have you heard from her?

BEN. We spoke a few times. Last week somehow I missed a call and she left a message. Broke my heart.

VINCENT. What did she say?

BEN. "Hey Me, it's Me." She said she wasn't coming back in the fall. Staying local. My first college romance shut down before we even got to Applebee's.

VINCENT. I need to hear some of that poetry.

BEN. No way.

VINCENT. Come on! Maybe I'll use some on Sara.

BEN. Well, I did start writing a new one in response to her voice mail.

VINCENT. Lay it on me. Don't worry, it's just us. No one else is here yet right?

BEN. *(Checking part of his screen.)* Nobody's in the waiting room. Yet. My dad and Effie should've been done by now but I guess the thing is running late.

VINCENT. What's the thing?

BEN. They're having their first streaming vestry meeting. Effie's part of the vestry.

VINCENT. What do they do, anyway? The vestry?

BEN. It's sort of like the board of directors. They make all church decisions. Money issues, upkeep… I think there's eight or nine people on it?

VINCENT. Anyway, hit me with some verses.

BEN. Ugh. Alright. Hold on.

> *He reaches behind him and pulls a pad out.*

This one is almost finished. It's got a rhythm to it.

> *He recites, hitting the rhymes.*

Hello it's Ben.
I'm writing again.
To my dream girl Trisha.
Lord knows, I miss ya.
We had to leave college,

37

But you have the knowledge.
My poems made it clear,
I was writing them all year,
They surely weren't vague.
Then you said yes, but then, the plague.

      Silence.

VINCENT. Wow, that definitely...rhymes.

BEN. They were all like that. I'm a pretty good rhymer. What do you think?

VINCENT. It's the worst shit I ever heard. But that's good news! It means this girl is into you for the right reasons, not just your poetry.

BEN. Thanks. I think.

VINCENT. Anyway, things with Sara were going well. It's like, I haven't had a serious relationship in a while and all the nice things about those few months we had years ago were coming back...but...

BEN. What?

VINCENT. It's all virtual. Like a video game.

BEN. Wait, she won't see you at all? In person?

VINCENT. Not until there's a vaccine, she says. It's not like I'm asking to get it on, I'm asking to take a walk! Masks on, whatever... I'll wear catcher's equipment if she wants. But nope. I said I'll walk across the street if she wants, bring my own plexiglass...nope. I mean, people are out now! Look at the protests! Things are opening up, clearly. But still, nothing for us. I'm sick of kissing my phone screen.

BEN. Not sure who has it worse, you or me. Sara's here, by the way. Keep that Trisha stuff between us, huh?

      A window appears. It's Sara...

SARA. Hello! Hello Ben! Hey Vin!

BEN. Hello.   VINCENT. What's up Sara.

SARA. I'm actually early. Can't believe it!

BEN. Why, are you late a lot?

SARA. I'm always late.   VINCENT. She's always late.

BEN. You guys are cute. Said the same thing at the same time.

SARA. Oh! So Vincent, I see you told Ben?

BEN. Um. Was I not supposed to know?

SARA. No, no, it's fine. It's not a secret. Our little reading in April led to some serious forgiveness on my part. We're keeping our social distance but getting closer in other ways. I call it our Phase Two Reopening.

VINCENT. I call it crazy.

BEN. Well congrats. At least *one* good thing came out of our play.

SARA. Why what happened? Something that wasn't good?

VINCENT. I saw it on the site. It was awesome. I mean, it was kind of bad awesome. Why didn't they leave it up there?

BEN. The vestry had us take it down.

SARA. What's a vestry?

VINCENT. I can answer that. The board of directors.

SARA. They didn't like it?

BEN. It was a bit of a controversy. The bishop hated it too.

VINCENT. Ouch! The bishop?

SARA. Is that your dad's boss?

BEN. Oh yes. There's like two ranks above my dad. Bishops and God.

VINCENT. What was wrong with our play?

SARA. I know. Me. It was me. As Jesus. A Jewish, female Jesus in your church's annual tradition. I should have passed on the role.

BEN. No, actually, that was the one element that got a positive response. Many of the older male parishioners stayed awake for the Passion for the first time in church history, and it was credited to, as one quite typically reserved parishioner put it, "the hot Jesus."

SARA. That's nice to hear.

VINCENT. What was the problem part?

BEN. Well folks, we sort of left out a key detail, remember? The whole Jesus coming back from the dead at the end?

VINCENT. Oh yeah.

BEN. Well some people tend to like that ending. Like, most of Western civilization. So suffice it to say, folks were not too happy

Jesus didn't resurrect, and I don't think it was only because he was hot and they wanted more screen time.

VINCENT. Is your dad in trouble?

BEN. They'll give him an earful but that's what they do in those meetings anyway. I've overheard a few when they used to have them in our living room. It's a cranky bunch.

VINCENT. Everyone seems so nice in church. That's weird to hear.

BEN. Well, they are nice. They're just protective of the place. They don't like change. I guess especially when it revokes miracles, and the basis of Christianity.

SARA. I feel so guilty. Major Jewish guilt.

VINCENT. I assume this doesn't bode well for our proposition.

SARA. Oh wow. Will it be up to these people?

BEN. Yes it will. My father liked your idea of starting a community theatre out of the church, and he thought maybe it could be sold to the vestry, but then the blowback from the Passion Play so...I don't know.

VINCENT. Ben, is Grace joining us? How is she feeling?

BEN. She's expected, yes. She wrote me that she feels ninety percent normal. Which is at least five percent more normal than she was to begin with.

SARA. We emailed. I told her to donate antibodies. It's sort of a moral imperative.

VINCENT. Well the important thing is that she recovered.

SARA. But she is *not* recovered from the acting bug! She told me she read the script I sent out as soon as it landed in her inbox. She loves it.

BEN. Sara, I hadn't read *Oedipus Rex* since high school! That is one nasty, bloody play. Are we sure that's the right choice for an inaugural production? If they let us?

VINCENT. Well you gotta love the relevance. A play set in a city with plague and protests where nothing will get better until the leader is gone.

SARA. I agree. It's perfect. That's exactly why Dodd chose it!

40

BEN. Dodd? Who is Dodd?

VINCENT. Dodd the Theatre Genius.

SARA. He's a director I worked with in Manhattan.

VINCENT. He runs his own big-time Manhattan company. Tell Ben about it, Sara. Tell Ben how big-time.

SARA. Dodd's very talented. Visionary.

VINCENT. His company offers unpaid, outdoor Shakespeare in parks with no permit.

SARA. He gets permits, that was just that one time. And the judge threw it out eventually.

VINCENT. That was the *one time* you worked with him. His "all-female" show. Except for himself.

SARA. *Taming of the Shrew.* It was great, actually. When it didn't rain.

VINCENT. This guy is also Sara's ex.

SARA. No he is not my ex. Just like you, Vincent, are not my ex.

BEN. Well you're currently dating Vincent. When you break up again, he'll be your ex, again.

VINCENT. Why isn't he considered an ex? See Ben, Sara and Dodd had what is called a "Showmance" in the biz.

SARA. Please, Vincent, enough.

BEN. What is *that*?

VINCENT. It is a showmance, I have been informed, when members of the cast or crew engage in intracompany sexual activity during the run of the show.

SARA. It happened opening night, okay? It was no big deal. And after each weeknight performance. It did also happen closing night. Then it was over.

VINCENT. But Dodd the Genius is now back in Sara's life. And hopefully all of ours too!

SARA. He's back virtually only.

VINCENT. Just like me. Thanks to our Passion Play! So we sort of do have a resurrection!

BEN. *Oedipus* was his idea?

41

SARA. I did a social media PR blast for our Passion Play and Dodd saw a post. He commented, "Congrats, Sara. That's totally intriguing!" He was so impressed that he asked me if the church might consider a resident theatre company, as he is looking to expand. I said I didn't know, but would have to ask you all. So I wrote you.

VINCENT. And here we are!

BEN. Right. And I'm so bored and depressed that I am ignoring the fact that nobody can really do theatre right now since the buildings are shut down. Just like church, and a great sophomore year at college, theatre is a communal event, and cannot happen without people.

SARA. That won't be forever, though!

BEN. True. But please don't get your hopes up. I live in the rectory. Grew up in it. I never left the church. Literally. So I learned things. Since I'm back now, in my childhood room, I have been exposed to information like the fact that this church is in the hole financially, an even deeper hole since lockdown as donations are way down. I know the vestry and the bishop hated our first show, and so I know, as I said, this is a long shot.

VINCENT. But you are hosting this meeting, so I guess you're hopeful.

BEN. I don't even know anymore. Maybe.

SARA. Listen, Dodd totally understands this church building is closed. But he looked it up on Google Maps and noted that we do have a nice, grassy...lawn.

BEN. We do have a lawn. The landscaper is quarantined as is my barber, so now the lawn and my hair look the same.

SARA. We could do theatre outside! Dodd's specialty! His concept is...you'll love this...well you know what? Let him tell you himself. I'll email him this meeting invite. Be right back.

VINCENT. Ah, Sara... I don't think we should plop a stranger here as we—

> Sara's window goes black, just reading "Sara: SAG-AFTRA Eligible."

Don't bring that dude on this call, Sara!

> Two more windows open: Effie and Fr. Theodore.

42

EFFIE. You all there?

VINCENT. Hey Effie.　　　　　　　　　BEN. Effie!

EFFIE. Father you on the air?

THEODORE. Just got on, Effie.

EFFIE. Father, if we ever meet in person again, I'm gonna stick that cane of hers right up the warden's butt.

THEODORE. Easy, Effie. She's an old woman.

EFFIE. How dare she talk to you like that.

THEODORE. I'm used to it.

EFFIE. Well I'm not. This is my third meeting on this vestry thing and I hate it.

THEODORE. Just please don't quit. I need you there.

EFFIE. They seem so warm and cuddly in the pews. In these meetings they're a bunch of uptight whiners. When I wasn't laughing at the folks, I was wantin' to throw a roundhouse at my computer.

THEODORE. Well I will say I was impressed with your technical skills. You stayed in frame the whole time.

EFFIE. Aw, I just needed a little practice. I'm a whiz now at this stuff. I can do anything. Split screen, sharing, mute…you name it, I can do it.

VINCENT. We've all had to learn. Sara and I have done a lot of experimenting.

THEODORE. Well anyway, hello everyone. Sorry we ran late. Vestry meeting was a bit…

EFFIE. A bit bullshit.

> *Something bumps her screen and it abruptly shoots its focus past her forehead onto the ceiling.*

BEN. Can't see your face Effie!

EFFIE. I know, I'm fixin' it!

> *She does.*

THEODORE. It was tense today. Effie's right. People are feeling the stress of the quarantine. I understand that. It's hard for people in very different ways.

EFFIE. How's it hard for that Colleen lady? How's her life changed? Husband still working, she doesn't. Never has. Never leaves their damn dumb big ugly house except when she's at church, complaining about something.

BEN. Wow, Effie. You're worked up.

EFFIE. I drank too. Whole meeting. Hope that's alright, Father.

THEODORE. I should have, too. Lord knows we have the wine here.

BEN. It was bad, Dad?

THEODORE. Nothing we haven't seen before. Even in a progressive church, people like to count on some things staying the same. Gives them comfort.

VINCENT. I heard our Passion Play was a problem.

THEODORE. Well, they appreciated the effort to put it online. But yes. Let's say our play got some bad reviews. I take full responsibility. I cut the resurrection! I don't know what came over me! One vestry member who shall remain nameless called what we did a "Jewish version where Jesus stayed dead."

EFFIE. That nameless vestry member is Bill McGlone. You know him. Meathead.

    Sara reappears.

THEODORE. Hello Sara.

SARA. Hello, Father.

THEODORE. Sara, you were the hit of the play, at least I can report that.

BEN. I told her, Dad.

THEODORE. They would like to book you for next year.

SARA. I'm available.

    Grace appears.

ALL. Hey Grace/Grace!

GRACE. Hi everyone! Hello!

SARA. You look great!

VINCENT. So glad you're feeling better.

EFFIE. Hear hear! We love you, honey!

44

GRACE. Thank you. Covid was so weird! Obviously as my cough got worse I couldn't help thinking that I had it. But then the cough stopped for a while. I had my Vitamin C, D, and Zinc infused teas every day, same time, and just slept and stayed hydrated. Thought it was a false alarm.

BEN. We all did.

GRACE. Father Theo was so sweet, he put me on the prayer list that first Sunday.

THEODORE. Oh that goes without saying, Grace. This is your church!

BEN. You were on the prayer lists every Sunday! We were worried, Grace.

GRACE. Well I thought whatever I had was gone, then one morning, I woke up with a raging headache, my eyes were red and my throat was dry... I went in and got the test. Boom. Positive.

SARA. Oh my God. So scary.

GRACE. Kicked my butt for two weeks. I barely ate. Just lay in bed watching old movies. My throat hurt so I stopped smoking the Mary Jane. Thank goodness for edibles. My taste is a little off now. It's weird. Water tastes like milk and milk tastes like eggs Benedict. But I'm lucky! It's gone. In fact, when I went back to get that test, it said I was negative!

VINCENT. That makes no sense! You had the virus! What a mess.

SARA. They don't know anything. We are totally lost.

THEODORE. So everyone, I know this meeting was supposed to be about starting a theatre here. And I do love the idea. I just wish I had some news to share with you. But I don't.

BEN. No news? Did you bring it up to the vestry?

EFFIE. So wait, what are we talking about? Having shows here? They did *Annie* over at Saint Paul's. My niece was in it. It was awful. She was cute. Eight-year-old. Not gonna be an actress, I'm pretty sure. I'm praying that was her last rodeo.

> A new window opens: the name "Dodd," over a posed-for photo of Dodd (30s–50s), looking artsy, thoughtful, and in control.

45

GRACE. Who's that guy?

THEODORE. Look, I am not the boss. I serve the parish. I just can't declare a thing is happening and it happens. I like this idea, as I said. I think it would be good. I just…think we're up against a few things. Like everyone else.

Dodd himself appears in his window.

GRACE. Hey, I think we got a Zoombomber!

EFFIE. What the hell is a Zoombomber?

GRACE. Someone who crashes the meeting. Just pops in uninvited! I learned about it on the news.

VINCENT. Nah, this is Sara's genius.

THEODORE. Hello. Can we help you?

DODD. I am Dodd. D-O-D-D. Artistic Director of the Al Fresco Shakespeare Company, Manhattan.

SARA. He's my guest, Father.

THEODORE. Hi Dodd. Welcome. I'm Father Theodore. Rector of the All Saints Episcopalian Church.

DODD. Thank you for having me.

THEODORE. So anyway, as much as I like this idea, I think we need to slow down, consider all that's going on in our world right now, and revisit this once things are more settled. At some point the church, the community, and the theatre stuff can maybe come together in a successful way.

DODD. Well if I may, sir, the theatre, church, and the community have an ancient connection. I believe it will come together because it has always come together. It is a very natural, very organic, and necessary synthesis.

VINCENT. Like a showmance.

SARA. Vincent, you're killing me.

DODD. From the beginning of time, the stories of mythology explained to us the world, our gods, and why what happens to us, happens to us. That's what you do in church, is it not? Your sacred job is to bring your flock together for their stories.

BEN. You know, you're right Dodd. Funny, I think the only theatre

46

I've ever been a part of is in church. Sunday school. And our Passion Play every year.

THEODORE. Folks, the parishioners complained about what I did to the Passion story, the bishop told me he was outraged. The vestry just let me have it. I think we gotta put this off awhile.

DODD. I thought a good choice would be *Oedipus the King*. Sophocles.

THEODORE. Sophocles. Wow. See, imagine I'm on that meeting just now, saying, "Hey, after our Jewish version of Jesus' death, we'd like to follow with the great pagan classic, where the king sleeps with his mother and pulls his eyes out."

DODD. We do it on your lawn. Outside. Just as it was in ancient Athens, which as we all know eventually suffered the great Plague of Athens and gave way to Oligarchy. I'll take Current American Crises for one hundred, Alex.

THEODORE. I'm sorry, we can't have a crowd here. Even if it's outside.

DODD. Answer: social distance and masks. We keep our audience on blankets six feet apart. As for masks? The ancients wore masks! Audience and the characters in masks! And as for those actors onstage, the ancients never had but a handful together at once—maybe two or three, we do the same. Theatre as it was, as it must be now, on your lawn. Our innovations to keep theatre alive. Maybe we'll get a feature in the *Times*.

SARA. That is so brilliant.

THEODORE. Look, I get it. All that stuff is cool. It's just not able to be done here.

BEN. But you're the rector, Dad! It's your church!

THEODORE. No, it's not. It's the parishioners' church!

EFFIE. *(Setting up another screen off-frame.)* Folks just a heads-up here, I got a Facebook Live wake I need to attend. Gonna try to do both here at once, double-screenin'…

GRACE. Oh, Effie I'm so sorry.

EFFIE. My brother's wife's dad. They're streaming it out of a funeral home in Brooklyn. Will probably be more fun than that vestry meeting.

THEODORE. By all means, Effie, just focus on that.

EFFIE. Nah, I don't want to leave y'all. I like this idea of doing some shows. I just wanted you to know why I was looking off to the side here at my phone. It already started.

GRACE. Effie, was it Covid?

EFFIE. Frank? He was 96 and a born smoker. Assumed room temperature while stretched out on his sofa watching *Wheel of Fortune*. Natural causes.

GRACE. Good. I mean... I don't know if I mean *good*.

EFFIE. Nah I know what you mean, darling. It was his time. He was a pisser, I liked him. But he was really old and losin' it. And like I said, he smoked like a steamboat. Keep talkin' everyone!

She pivots to look at a screen off-frame.

DODD. I am prepared to direct the project at a reduced fee.

THEODORE. So folks, the vestry is interested in promoting the church, in nurturing our congregation in a Christian manner. If the church itself is used for other activities it should be an extension of worship in some way. As much as I admire all the world's mythologies, I don't think *Oedipus* advances our mission.

EFFIE. *(At other screen.)* Closed casket. Looks like they got a dozen mourners or so in there, max. Standing all apart. Weird.

BEN. Dad, I remember Sunday school. When we lived in Delaware, your first assignment as rector.

GRACE. Aw. Cute little Ben in Sunday school! I can totally see it!

SARA. I went to Hebrew school. Temple Beth Torah. Dated a guy named Steven.

VINCENT. Was it a Hebrewmance?

SARA. Big-time.

EFFIE. *(At other screen.)* Priest is making comments on Frank's life. I always wonder if priests really know this much about the dead guy or do they get a script. Always sounds the same. People are typing stuff. Where's that coming from?

BEN. It's called a chat. See? You're still learning!

EFFIE. *(At other screen.)* I can barely see it.

> *She squints to read.*

Frank was a great guy. I'm gonna get a headache doing this.

THEODORE. Ben, of course I remember you in Sunday school. Mom was your teacher.

BEN. Well I remember the way she taught the stories. She made us act them out. Adam and Eve, Cain and Abel, Noah's Ark...

DODD. Ah! Now there's an idea! Medieval Mystery Plays. Those were outdoor as well!

GRACE. Mysteries? Like, Whodunits?

DODD. These were festival skits that reenacted stories of the Bible. That's what she was doing, it sounds like. Your mother sounds intriguing. Is she still with us?

THEODORE. She's downstairs making cutlets.

BEN. We would split up into groups and do the plays in the classroom. It was fun. And I never forgot those stories.

DODD. The trade guilds of the medieval towns would do the same. It really was the first kind of community theatre, come to think of it. The carpenters would put on the story of Noah, or the bakers the Last Supper. The people of the community would see their friends and townspeople onstage, playing out the stories they grew up with. Hold on, I have a book in my private library.

> *He leans out of view for a moment.*

VINCENT. Private library?

SARA. *(Trying to whisper.)* It's three or four stacks of books around his desk.

BEN. Dad, maybe the vestry would like if we did something like that. Bible plays.

> *Dodd returns.*

DODD. Here you are. Medieval Mystery Plays. Here's how Creation begins:

> *He reads.*

I am gracious and great, God without beginning,
I am maker unmade, all of might is in me;

I am life and way unto wealth and winning,
I am foremost and first, all I bid shall be.

EFFIE. *(Re: her other screen.)* Sounds like this priest.

SARA. Very nicely read, Dodd.

DODD. Thank you, Sara. Stentorian style.

EFFIE. *(Back to the group.)* I don't see that puttin' butts in seats. It's a little stiff. Can't we update it?

DODD. How do you mean?

EFFIE. I don't know, give it a little punch. Spice it up.

DODD. A modern adaptation! Yes. I can modernize the text and, of course, direct the show to spotlight any relevant social motifs. I would ask that I be credited with the adaptation in the program.

VINCENT. Wait. Hold on. Hold on. As a founding member of this nonexistent theatre company, I'd like to propose an idea. Here it is. Bible plays. Adapted for a modern audience.

SARA. Dodd just said that, Vinny. Are you feeling alright?

VINCENT. Yes I am. And with all due respect to Dodd, I know a great "in-house" poet, a member of this very church, who can make this stuff sing with a modern glory. It'll be the *Hamilton* of Bible plays...

SARA. Ha! Who is that? You?

VINCENT. All in favor give thumbs-up.

> *Vincent, Effie, and Grace post the "thumbs-up" emoji. Ben stares at the screen, frozen.*

BEN. Vincent, who is this...*in-house* poet?

VINCENT. Thumbs-up, Ben! Let's see it!

EFFIE *(At other screen.)* Oh God, they're starting a whole slideshow of Frank's life to music. Now everyone's typing in how sad they are and how great he looks.

VINCENT. Come on, Ben. You're one for one. Batting a thousand. She did say yes!

THEODORE. What's that mean? Who said yes to what?

BEN. *(Wanting to distract.)* Nothing. Nobody! Okay! Yes! Yes! Thumbs-up!

Ben gives thumbs-up. Dodd and Sara follow.

VINCENT. Unanimous!

GRACE. And maybe it'll repair your relationship with God, Father Theo!

THEODORE. It's the bishop who's mad, and the vestry. Not God. Look around. These days I don't think He'd be concerned with whatever I'm doing. Though who knows.

DODD. May I add one suggestion, since it seems you're going up against a hostile authority. And I'm used to that.

SARA. Please, yes. Thank you, Dodd.

DODD. We do a kind of backers' audition.

SARA. Brilliant. Very smart.

DODD. Before presenting all forty-five Mystery plays at once.

THEODORE. What?! Forty-five?

DODD. We present a sampling of the first few. A high-quality showcase of the material. Then they invest.

THEODORE. Nobody's *investing*. They would be *allowing* use of the church property.

DODD. We rehearse the first couple scenes, edit our best takes, then send it to the producers.

VINCENT. You mean the vestry.

EFFIE. *(At other screen.)* Jeez, Frank's in his twenties in these. This is gonna take all night. They can tell if I'm watchin' right? This Facebook Live business?

BEN. They'll probably only know you're there if you comment. You may want to comment early and comment late so it looks like you've been on the whole time.

EFFIE. I gotcha. What do I even say? This is depressing.

> *She turns to the group.*

Do me a favor, guys. When my wake happens, do a slideshow like this, but let me pick the pictures. Father, I'll send you what I want.

THEODORE. I don't want to think about your wake, Effie.

EFFIE. But you never know, Father. No matter what you do...good or bad…you're bound to kick it at some point, then all you got is your wake and slideshow.

DODD. The Greeks called that your Kleos, your immortal reputation, that for which you will be remembered.

EFFIE. This Dodd guy's a hoot. So what are we doin' Father? A little show for the vestry?

THEODORE. Well it does sound like something they could possibly approve.

VINCENT. Alright everyone, give my poet a week. I'll email you when the scripts are ready.

GRACE. Yay! Can't wait!

EFFIE. *(To other screen, typing.) Poor…Frank.* There's my comment.

DODD. So I understand I will be directing?

VINCENT. That's wrong. I will be directing.

SARA. Dodd should direct. He's a professional.

DODD. Perhaps we should discuss this. Sara, would you give us the room?

SARA. Sure.

> *Sara's window goes out. Grace waves, then signs off, as does Father Theo. Dodd, Vincent, Effie, and Ben are left onscreen. Effie watches her other screen.*

BEN. Vincent?

VINCENT. Yeah Ben.

BEN. I'm the poet?

VINCENT. You know it.

BEN. Vincent.

VINCENT. Yes, poet.

BEN. My poems are really bad. I know that.

EFFIE. *(To other screen.)* Look at him. Just a regular guy. I barely know this man, and I'm sad. Death is sad.

DODD. And frightening. And incomprehensible. It is that undiscovered country from whose bourn no traveler returns. Except when they do return, as in *Hamlet.*

EFFIE. What a hoot. Anyway, night, y'all.

BEN, VINCENT, and DODD. Night.

Effie disappears.

VINCENT. Ben.

BEN. Yeah?

VINCENT. Get to work, my lover. And send Trisha, who I'm sure still misses ya, the link when we're recording it.

BEN. No way. Are you crazy?

VINCENT. Let her see her poet in action!

BEN. That is out of the question.

DODD. It's Vincent, correct?

VINCENT. It's Vincent. Correct.

DODD. I think you should play Adam to Sara's Eve.

VINCENT. I think you should play the devil.

DODD. Happy to. He's in the second scene. A dynamic role.

BEN. And I think you guys should both direct. I'll be too anxious and embarrassed to be much help. Dodd you do the one Vincent is in. Vincent you do the one Dodd's in.

DODD. I accept. Co-directors. I love collaboration. And threesomes. See you at rehearsal.

Dodd's window goes black.

VINCENT. Ben?

BEN. Yeah.

VINCENT. Get to work.

Blackout.

Scene 2

Same.

A week later. Six windows are open; Ben, Vincent, and Dodd are on in their windows onscreen.

Grace's, Sara's, and Effie's screens are open, but they're not there.

DODD. *(Arms wide apart, crucifix-style.)* And of course in the real thing, outside, we start the show towards dusk, so that when we get to the resurrection, I would be lit only by streetlamps on the cross, with Sara as Mary Magdalene weeping at my feet.

VINCENT. Dodd, hang on there. Ben?

BEN. Yeah?

VINCENT. Sorry to bring it up again. I'm just saying, this is your last chance. We've run it a few times now, it's good as it's gonna get. We're recording this time. Send her the invite!

BEN. I told you. I'm not doing it. I'll never see her again anyway.

DODD. What is this about?

VINCENT. You don't know that, Ben!

BEN. I don't know that the play reads as well aloud as it does on the page.

VINCENT. Oh I would say it's the same aloud as on paper, brother. Despite that, I say invite her.

BEN. Maybe I'll send her the finished product. Or invite her to the real show.

DODD. Are you considering inviting someone to observe right now? Is it a critic? Or a journalist of any kind?

VINCENT. What if there is no finished product? What if this is the only run we get? You told me your dad is extremely skeptical. He's gonna watch this right now and if he thinks this will only piss off the vestry even more, that's the end of it.

BEN. I know. He's been miserable lately.

VINCENT. Send her the link! If she shows up, it means you guys aren't over!

DODD. This is a romantic question. I see.

BEN. She's shy though. And she doesn't know anyone here.

VINCENT. She barely knows *you*! Send it!

DODD. Send it, Ben. I agree with Vincent here. There is nothing to ignite the forces of Eros like the theatre. Whoever this is, I assure you, after she sees you at work, she will surrender.

VINCENT. Is that how it works in Manhattan, Dodd?

DODD. It cannot be helped.

BEN. Okay! Okay! I'm sending it.

> *He presses some keys. Sara appears in her window, sanitizing her hands.*

There it goes. The die is cast. It's so last-minute, hopefully she won't see it.

> *Grace arrives at her screen.*

SARA. Oh, you mean the girl from school? Is she gonna watch?

BEN. You told Sara?

GRACE. Told Sara what?

BEN. That was private, Vincent. Sara, please don't mention this to anyone else.

GRACE. Oh don't worry! Vincent told everyone.

> *Effie returns to her screen.*

EFFIE. I'm back! Break over?

VINCENT. Break's over.

EFFIE. Well let's knock this sucker out.

> *A ring is heard from a cell phone. Dodd looks down in his frame, and silences it.*

DODD. I must take this call. Sorry everyone. Be right back.

> *Dodd mutes himself and takes the call. We see him on a business-looking call, but don't hear him.*

VINCENT. Ben, is your dad gonna watch? I want him to see what we've worked on.

BEN. Oh yeah. Hold on.

He turns off-frame and yells.

DAD! We're starting!

No response.

DAD!

Dodd ends his call and unmutes himself.

DODD. Sorry everyone. That was L.A. Told them I'd call back.

SARA. L.A.! Cool. Business?

DODD. Yes. Wells Fargo. I've missed two Visa payments.

VINCENT. Alright, when Father Theo comes on, let's do this for real. Ben, we ready to record?

GRACE. Vincent, I love how you've stepped into this director role. Love seeing you take charge.

DODD. Co-director. And I too have enjoyed working with you Vincent. Hard to believe you haven't done this before. But as Shakespeare wrote, "some have greatness thrust upon 'em."

VINCENT. It's one hundred percent sexual frustration.

DODD. I've never had that.

Father Theodore appears in a new window.

THEODORE. I'm here.

He looks worn.

I am still...here.

VINCENT. Okay. Is everyone in attendance? Ben?

BEN. Looks like it.

VINCENT. Anyone else...signing on?

BEN. Everyone's here, Vincent. I'm ready to record.

DODD. Okay cast and crew, so I think we made great progress today. At this point I'll put it simply: Keep up the pace.

VINCENT. The pace. The pace. Ben?

BEN. Yeah, Vincent.

VINCENT. You all set up to record the first one?

BEN. Told you that already.

VINCENT. Has anyone else…signed on? In the waiting room?

EFFIE. Who else is signing on? We're all here!

GRACE. Ben's lady friend.

EFFIE. Oh! The girl Vincent told me about?

BEN. We're all here. Everyone is ready. Let's record it.

DODD. Places everybody. Scene One. *Creation…* God, Adam. Eve.

VINCENT. *(Teasingly.)* Eve, made to be my wife.

BEN. Alright folks, like last time, for technical reasons I need that little breath pause before your first line.

DODD. Then keep the pace, and emphasize the couplet ends with a rising inflection. Attack the rhyme.

BEN. I worked hard on those rhymes. Ready when you are.

VINCENT. Ben? Everyone…everyone…is here?

BEN. We're all here. Stop asking that. Please, we can go.

DODD. Okay. Here we go. The story of Creation. Genesis.

BEN. *(Looking down, off-frame.)* Holy cow!

GRACE. What's wrong?

BEN. The waiting room.

VINCENT. She's here. She's here! Let her in!

GRACE. Let her in!

THEODORE. I'm sorry, who is this?

VINCENT. We have a guest. A lover of poetry.

BEN. Oh my God, I'm freaking out.

SARA. Relax, Ben.

Ben is reading something on his screen.

EFFIE. What's happening?

BEN. *(Smiling.)* Ha. She's…she's very clever. Her username says, "Me."

THEODORE. Who's "Me"?

VINCENT. It's a long and squeamish story.

GRACE. Let her in, Ben! She's just in time!

Ben takes a deep breath.

BEN. Here goes. Everybody be cool. She's shy.

A beat, and a new window appears. It is black. It reads: "Me."
A silence. Ben attempts to be charming.

Hi there, Me. Thanks for checking us out.

Silence.

She's muted.

He speaks to the window.

Thank you for being here. Sorry for the late notice!

A pause. Then, the thumbs-up emoji appears on the black
screen. Everyone cheers.

VINCENT. Alright! Let's hit this hard and knock that vestry out folks!

They all cheer again. Ben looks nervous. Theodore leans in, as
if having a touch of renewed interest. Everyone gathers their
scripts before them.

BEN. Alright. Ready? Recording!

DODD. Effie, or God...you're at the dawn of the universe. Go.

EFFIE. *(As God.) A god's gotta work. That's what I say.*
Can't sit around, all-knowing, all day.
What good is my power and all this might,
In boring old Heaven, alone all night?
No stories to follow, no drama enjoyed.
I like being perfect, but not unemployed.
So I rolled up my sleeves, made angels in flight,
Put planets in the sky, a moon for the night,
A sun for the day, and earth, trees, and grass;
Thriving beasts, bugs, fish, fowl, and ass.

She laughs, drops her character.

Ha! Ass! I made some ass too over these last few months. Lord have
mercy. All that cheese!

BEN. I'll cut that. And God means donkeys there, Effie. Keep going
please.

EFFIE. Sorry.

She gets back into character...

These animals thrive, but they don't seem to care

That I gave them all this, their lives, food, the air...
I see no beast that's worshipping me!
They just eat, sleep, hump, poop lots, and pee.
The world needs another, my friend, so to speak,
Who'll care for the place, and work all week.
From my own shape and likeness, just not quite so great,
I shall make man, like a god, but second-rate.
I'll give all my gifts, all but one—life eternal.
If good, they'll come to Heaven, if bad, Hell infernal.

   Effie, as God, raises a hand.

Rise up, you dirt, flesh, bone, thought, sensation!
This sixth workday now, come forth...my creation!

THEODORE. *(Smiling.)* That...wasn't bad. I must admit.

DODD. Thank you.

BEN. Dad, we're recording.

DODD. And now, enter Adam!

VINCENT. *(As Adam.) Check me out! I got life! From nowhere, it's*
  a shock!
Now what does God want me to do with this...

   He looks down at his lap.

...existence?

THEODORE. Jesus.

BEN. Shhh!

EFFIE. *(As God.) Adam shall know woman, the world's first relation.*
Wait till you see her, you'll be full of erection!

THEODORE. Woah! Woah!

DODD. Sorry. Effie, let's double back. That's supposed to be "elation"
not "erection." We went over this multiple times.

EFFIE. You got it.

BEN. Rolling.

EFFIE. *(As God.) You shall know woman, the world's first relation.*
Wait till you see her, you'll be full of erection. Elation!
I'll use a nice rib from the side of your chest,
To build her upon—so it's sort of incest.

59

But don't let that trouble you, you'll have kids with ease,
And live in this garden. Just lay off that tree. Please!
Adam and Eve it will be. That's what I'll call you.
Now enjoy yourselves, but remember, don't fall, you!

   She drops her character.

Ha! But oh they fall, though, don't they!

DODD. Sara, lovely…you're on! Eve lives!

SARA. *(As Eve.) Look at this world! Such beauty and peace!*

VINCENT. *(As Adam.) A heckuva place to hit the sack and increase!*

SARA. *(As Eve.) Come on, let's go slow, get out there and mingle.*
We just got created, and we're no longer single?

EFFIE. *(As God.) They're worth my effort. I can already see,*
But let me add one last thing, then you're free.
I'm to be worshipped, for what I've done here.
Every day, every hour, every minute all year.
Enjoy all the goods, have rule over all,
On Earth that is, and that, that is all.
I said it before but I'll repeat, so I'm clear.
Besides worshipping me, there's another rule here.
Don't touch that apple, or fruit, whatever it be.
That juicy, ripe, round thing, hanging off that short tree.
Don't ask any questions, I'll answer them not.
Just do what I say, and you'll keep what you got.

SARA. *(As Eve.) Then why put the tree there? If it's so bad to eat?*
Why even tempt us, if you know we might cheat?

VINCENT. *(As Adam.) Eve, so many questions. Just leave it alone.*
Just kiss me, for real, not over the phone.

   He drops his character, proud.

I added that.

EFFIE. *(As God.) Don't squabble, my dears, don't ruin the mood.*
Take a step back, get a look, you're both spankin' nude.

DODD. This is wonderful work. Terrific ensemble.

GRACE. It's a work of genius.

THEODORE. This is all about sex! I can't show them this!

60

BEN. Quiet! Please! Still rolling!

DODD. Continue Sara, my dear!

SARA. *(As Eve.) Of the two humans here, the girl's more attractive.*

EFFIE. *(As God.) It's true my dear Eve, but you'll be interactive.*

VINCENT. *(As Adam.) Oh I see how it works. Let's give it a go!*

SARA. *(As Eve.) Chill out, brand-new man, like I said, we go slow.*

EFFIE. *(As God.) Six days this all took. I'm a god, but I'm beat.*
Day seven I'll rest, go back up to my seat.
They please me already. It's good! I just knew it.
And if they fail me, by flood, fire…plague…I'll redo it.

> *A pause.*

DODD. And…scene.

> *Everyone but Theodore applauses, cheers enthusiastic comments. They are excited.*

That was good. Very, very good. I love directing.

BEN. Pretty tight!

EFFIE. What do you think, Father?

THEODORE. I…I…you all were all lovely, I…it just sounds…I mean, it's funny. I know that it's funny but…is this…making fun? I mean…I'm a bit confused.

DODD. Well, if I may, sir.

THEODORE. Please, Genius.

DODD. In their inception somewhere early 15th Century, some irreverence was part of the point. These were kind of a chance to blow off some steam for the people. Sort of see things from…the human point of view. So yes. They're a little… I mean, their lives were really hard and…full of sickness, violence, endless labor. Sometimes it sort of seemed God was…not so loving. Or not even there anymore, maybe. They didn't necessarily think that but…it was hard sometimes not to…think that. Who could blame them?

> *A pause. Theodore is grave.*

THEODORE. This has no chance with the vestry.

VINCENT. Why don't we ask our guest what she thinks?

BEN. Vincent...please don't?

He addresses the "Me" window.

You don't have to answer.

GRACE. So, as an objective onlooker, what do you think of our play?

A pause. After a moment, the thumbs-up emoji appears in the "Me" window. Everyone cheers. Ben is uplifted.

BEN. Okay. Okay! Let's...let's move to the second scene! Let's keep rolling!

VINCENT. The Fall of Lucifer. So God sits on his throne, and take it away Effie!

EFFIE. *(As God.) I'm the head god in charge, I'm doing just fine,*
And behind me, my angels, an order of nine.
They'll all live beneath me, I'll put them to task,
Between Earth and back, whatever I ask.
Bring a plague, let's say, or storm when I might,
They got wings, flowing hair, they're a heavenly sight.

BEN. And Lucifer stand by...

VINCENT. Dodd that's you man.

DODD. I'm at places.

EFFIE. *(As God.) And you, brightest angel, you, my right hand,*
I hereby make you second-in-command.
You'll stand nearby, oversee the rest,
I picked you, Lucifer, because, Hell, you're the best.
There's something about you I find very good,
I have no lieutenant, but maybe I should.
I gave you that name, the bearer of light,
'Cause a warm fuzzy feeling comes with you in sight.
So relax, Heaven's home, move in right away.
You have my full love, don't piss it away.

VINCENT. And God moves off...take it Dodd!

DODD. *(As Lucifer, like a pro.) Well heck, that was something. What a*
shot in the arm!
I hadn't thought of myself having that kind of charm.
I've tried to be good, to be helpful and kind,
But now, with that praise, there's more on my mind.

I am kinda bright, I am kinda strong.
God calls me the best, He's God, can't be wrong!
His praises were loud, His praises verbose,
I wonder if He's thinking, "Keep this guy close."
I wonder if my greatness shook God to His core,
I may consider my options some more.

VINCENT. Here the deluded, self-involved Lucifer turns to a passing angel. Grace, stand by!

GRACE. I'm here!

DODD. *(As Lucifer.) Hey you, angel there, a quick question, sir,*
Who's more attractive? The boss? Or Lucifer?
Don't answer just yet—but let me explain.
I'm considering an overthrow, or do you think that's insane?

GRACE. *(As Angel.) And if you're successful, I'd sure like to serve you.*
I detest my low rank, I hope I don't unnerve you.
The complaint I have is just job-related
He sent me down there to that world He created.
My circle is low, too close to the Earth,
I want to work higher, feelin' the mirth.

DODD. *(As Lucifer.) Back me up and you'll see, what promotion*
  you'll know,
If I take His seat, you won't work far below.

GRACE. *(As Angel.) Your plan sounds like fairness! No classes! No levels!*
Free Heaven for all, for every angel, all revels.

  She drops her character.

Kinda sounds like Bernie Sanders. Funny. I'm acting with the devil and I'm feelin' the "Bern," get it?

BEN. Recording! Stay on the lines, please. Keep going, Devil!

DODD. *(As Lucifer.) This rebellion might happen. You just gave me*
  the nod!
I don't have to serve Him, I myself can be God!

VINCENT. Great! We'll have God's window reappear and…Lucifer is busted. Effie, get that son of a bitch!

EFFIE. *(As God.) Oh yeah Lucifer? Sitting in my seat?*

DODD. *(As Lucifer.) Somethin' tells me I'm 'bout to feel the heat.*

EFFIE. *(As God.) You, rule the world? You really think so?*

DODD. *(As Lucifer.) Who me? No. No. No.*
No No No, No No No!

VINCENT. Then Dodd's in Hell! Flames! Agony!

BEN. I'll add all that in post!

VINCENT. Now we bring God back in…

BEN. Clouds, blue sky, rainbows!

EFFIE. *(As God.) Was it their hearts? Or was it their brains?*
What gave them ambition that's now brought them pains?
My wrath will go with them, in woe they will dwell,
Whoever else has such thoughts can meet them in Hell.

  Silence.

GRACE. Wow. These stories kinda make it seem like people…don't have a chance.

  Another silence.

VINCENT. And…that's what we got to show, right Ben? That's what we rehearsed.

BEN. That's what we got. Cut!

VINCENT. Awesome job, everyone! Way to stay on the lines!

DODD. Excellent pace.

BEN. Thank you all, thank you!

SARA. Great writing Ben! Resident playwright, I'd say!

BEN. Dad, the plan is that we edit that all together and…what do you think? Will the vestry go for it? It's the Bible! It's the stories of the Bible!

THEODORE. Oh, folks. That was very… But I don't know if…

EFFIE. The vestry sees this, Father. I insist! If that Colleen has a problem she can take it up with me.

THEODORE. I'm just not sure that the tone—

BEN. Dad, please!

SARA. We should leave you all to talk. I thought it was great. I'll ask your friend, Ben. What did you think?

BEN. Aw, please leave her out of it, I don't want to put her on the spot!

SARA. Objective observer! What's your verdict?

A pause. The "Me" screen is silent, then the thumbs-up emoji appears. They cheer again.

THEODORE. Who *is* that?

VINCENT. Father, please. Please give us…a chance. These are great stories.

DODD. Congratulations all. It was a pleasure working with you. Call me when the company is established. I'd love to program a full season.

SARA. Dodd, thank you. Call you later.

VINCENT. Why are you calling him later?

SARA. Vincent, please!

DODD. Theatre plans. Only theatre plans! I promise. Sara, I'll call after I shower.

His window disappears.

EFFIE. I gotta run. I gotta be in my kitchen. Good night all. And nobody worry. The vestry will see this and know they have no choice but to give us a big green light.

Her window closes.

SARA. Thank you. Again. Ben, once again, great work with the plays. As an actress these days, I kind of needed this. Glad you all found me.

BEN. Thanks Sara, means a lot.

VINCENT. When are we meeting tonight darling, or "Sara Lovely"?

SARA. Eight.

VINCENT. Can't wait. I'll be at my desk!

SARA. So will I.

Vincent's window disappears with Sara's.
Only Ben, Theodore, and the black screen, "Me," remain. A pause.

THEODORE. Ben. This won't work, Ben.

BEN. Ah, Dad. Do you mind if we talk offline? I want to speak to…my guest. I may as well introduce you. We met just a few weeks before… Trisha, this is my—

A ping is heard. A pause as Ben checks his phone.

Wait a minute.

THEODORE. What?

BEN. This is weird.

> *He reads, from off-frame.*

Hey it's Me. Saw your text just now. Is it over?

> *Silence.*

THEODORE. What's wrong?

> *Ben gazes, confounded, toward his lens.*

BEN. So wait…that's not you?

> *Silence. We hear another ping from Ben's phone. He looks off-frame at it, reads.*

Just pulled up to my house. Did I miss your rehearsal? Would love to attend.

> *Silence. He looks up again into his lens.*
> *Silence.*

THEODORE. Who are you talking to?

> *Ben continues to stare into his lens. A pause.*

BEN. Are you a Zoombomber?

> *Beat.*

Hello?

THEODORE. What does that mean? Please tell me what's happening?

BEN. How did you know to call yourself "Me"?

> *Silence.*

Do you know me?

> *A silence. Finally, the thumbs-up emoji appears in the "Me" window.*

Who are you?

> *Silence. No answer.*

Nobody else had this link.

> *Silence.*

THEODORE. Ben, end this call.

BEN. Wait.

THEODORE. Ben, now.

66

BEN. Wait, Dad.

> *Pause.*

Do you…do you know our church?

> *Pause. Thumbs-up emoji in the "Me" window.*

Do you…are we…

> *Something occurs to him.*

Do you like what we just did?

> *Pause. Thumbs-up emoji in the "Me" window. Silence.*

THEODORE. Ben?

> *Ben is silent.*

Who is that?

> *The "Me" window looms. Ben, confounded, suspicious, but calm, gazes into his lens. He leans in, as if looking closer at the window. Theodore is beginning to be agitated.*

Ben. Please answer me.

BEN. *(Gingerly.)* I'm…gonna…step away…in case…so you can… I'm…

> *Ben's window goes black. All that is left is Theodore and the "Me" window.*

THEODORE. I don't understand… Is someone there?

> *Pause. Thumbs-up emoji in the "Me" window.*

Okay. Okay. And you… You know us here? You know…who I am?

> *Pause. Thumbs-up emoji in the "Me" window. Theodore is growing steadily more irritated.*

Ah. Okay. So, I wonder…just wondering, whoever this is, I'm wondering…if you know what I do. I wonder… I wonder if, I might as well ask, if you know how I feel right now.

> *Pause. A thumbs-up emoji in the "Me" window.*

Ah. Well. You know how I feel? Helpless. Really. But thank you. I feel…like there's really not much for me to do. Weeks and weeks now I've… I can't really think of what else I'm supposed to… Can you tell me? What would you suggest? Should we do nothing? Just…wait…? For the horrors to be over? There's so many. So many right now. Is this doing any good? My job? Is that my job? Am I doing any good...any good at all? The vestry doesn't seem to think so. What do you think? Am I doing my job?

Silence. Then, a thumbs-up emoji in the "Me" window.

Ah.

Theodore gasps in relief, or dismay. He grabs at breath.

I appreciate that. Whoever you—

Something significant, but simple, occurs to him. He stares. A silence. Then, in a gentle, deeply respectful tone...

One more question. That's all. I promise. Is what Grace said before... do people...do people have a chance?

Longest pause yet. Then, the thumbs-up emoji in the "Me" window. After a moment, the window vanishes. Father Theodore is alone in his window a moment. He might cry, he might smile. Meekly, he utters...

Thank you. Oh...thank you.

Ben's window reopens.

BEN. Dad?

No answer.

Dad?

THEODORE. Ben.

Pause.

BEN. What do you think?

No response.

What do we do?

THEODORE. We...edit those...plays. And send them to the vestry. Then until this is all over...we...however we can, get everyone together. And we...see each other, however we can. And we... we tell the stories. However we can. And wait.

Long hold on father and son.
Blackout.

End of Play

PROPERTY LIST
(Use this space to create props lists for your production)

SOUND EFFECTS
(Use this space to create sound effects lists for your production)

Dear reader,

Thank you for supporting playwrights by purchasing this acting edition! You may not know that Dramatists Play Service was founded, in 1936, by the Dramatists Guild and a number of prominent play agents to protect the rights and interests of playwrights. To this day, we are still a small company committed to our partnership with the Guild, and by proxy all playwrights, established and aspiring, working in the English language.

Because of our status as a small, independent publisher, we respectfully reiterate that this text may not be distributed or copied in any way, or uploaded to any file-sharing sites, including ones you might think are private. Photocopying or electronically distributing books means both DPS and the playwright are not paid for the work, and that ultimately hurts playwrights everywhere, as our profits are shared with the Guild.

We also hope you want to perform this play! Plays are wonderful to read, but even better when seen. If you are interested in performing or producing the play, please be aware that performance rights must be obtained through Dramatists Play Service. This is true for *any* public performance, even if no one is getting paid or admission is not being charged. Again, playwrights often make their sole living from performance royalties, so performing plays without paying the royalty is ultimately a loss for a real writer.

This acting edition is the **only approved text for performance.** There may be other editions of the play available for sale from other publishers, but DPS has worked closely with the playwright to ensure this published text reflects their desired text of all future productions. If you have purchased a revised edition (sometimes referred to as other types of editions, like "Broadway Edition," or "[Year] Edition"), that is the only edition you may use for performance, unless explicitly stated in writing by Dramatists Play Service.

Finally, this script cannot be changed without written permission from Dramatists Play Service. If a production intends to change the script in any way—including casting against the writer's intentions for characters, removing or changing "bad" words, or making other cuts however small—without permission, they are breaking the law. And, perhaps more importantly, changing an artist's work. Please don't do that!

We are thrilled that this play has made it into your hands. We hope you love it as much as we do, and thank you for helping us keep the American theater alive and vital.

Note on Songs/Recordings, Images, or Other Production Design Elements

Be advised that Dramatists Play Service, Inc., neither holds the rights to nor grants permission to use any songs, recordings, images, or other design elements mentioned in the play. It is the responsibility of the producing theater/organization to obtain permission of the copyright owner(s) for any such use. Additional royalty fees may apply for the right to use copyrighted materials.

For any songs/recordings, images, or other design elements mentioned in the play, works in the public domain may be substituted. It is the producing theater/organization's responsibility to ensure the substituted work is indeed in the public domain. Dramatists Play Service, Inc., cannot advise as to whether or not a song/arrangement/recording, image, or other design element is in the public domain.

NOTES
(Use this space to make notes for your production)